EVIDENCE!

HOW DR. JOHN SNOW SOLVED THE MYSTERY OF CHOLERA

DEBORAH
HOPKINSON

ILLUSTRATED BY
NIK HENDERSON

ALFRED A. KNOPF NEW YORK

London, late August, 1854

Welcome to Broad Street, in hot, stinky old London.

Factories spew yellow smoke. Piles of horse dung line the streets.
Sewage and human waste fill cesspools in yards and cellars.

Everyone's thirsty. Annie Lewis must wait her turn
to fetch a pail of water from the Broad Street pump.

Annie lives just steps away, with her parents, older brother, and sickly baby sister. They crowd into a single room in a house of twenty people. They don't have showers, indoor toilets, or sinks with running water.

On Thursday, a man
in the house falls ill; on
Friday, he passes away.

The sad news—and the sickness—explodes like wildfire.
Scared neighbors flee or stay inside. For others it's too late.
Cholera has come to Broad Street.

Priests and doctors rush from bed to bed. But there is no cure for cholera, no way to stop its spread. Besides, the stench is everywhere. And all the doctors think bad, smelly air is to blame for this disease.

All doctors, except one.

Here's Dr. John Snow now, on Sunday evening.
He looks like a gentleman, but he grew up poor, the
oldest of nine children. John hasn't forgotten that.
He's been a doctor to the queen, but he cares about
science and regular people, not riches. He often gives
his services for free to those in need.

Tonight, John's not here to see a patient. He's
on the hunt for clues. Because John is a detective:
a medical detective.

John is investigating cholera. He's been chasing it for years. Whenever the disease breaks out in London, John's there—observing, making notes, poring over street maps. His goal? To figure out what causes cholera—and stop it in its tracks.

John has seen that cholera causes horrible stomach problems—vomiting and diarrhea. That's led him to believe something people swallow is making them sick. *But what?*

John has also noticed that cholera doesn't affect whole cities at once. It breaks out in clusters, bubbling up like blisters. John wants to know: *What links these cases together?*

Here on Broad Street, hundreds have been struck down in just a few days. It seems unlikely that everyone ate the exact same food.

But maybe, just maybe . . . they drank the same water!

And so John's steps lead him to the heart of the outbreak, where Annie and her thirsty neighbors draw water from the well.

He stops before the Broad Street pump.

We can guess he's thinking of paths and patterns; he may already be making a map of the outbreak in his head.

We can even imagine his thoughts: *This time! This time, I will finally crack the case. This time, I'll get the evidence I need to prove my bold hypothesis: Cholera is spread not by air, but by water.*

John pulls out a small bottle from his pocket and fills it. Not a drop will touch his lips. Instead, he takes it home, a ten-minute walk away.

John sees nothing unusual under his microscope.
The tools in his lab aren't powerful enough to reveal the
tiny organisms we now know were there (*vibrio cholerae*).

Even though he can't see any
evidence, John won't give up.
He'll need another way to show
that people who got sick drank
water from the pump.

But the bad-air theory has been around for years. People smell the stench; they see piles of poop and rotting vegetables. They won't believe John's theory that something invisible is spreading the disease. *Not without more proof.*

To change how the world
thinks, John will need a different
kind of evidence.
    He'll have to visit families,
ask questions, and gather facts.
    He'll have to use his feet.

John will have to work fast, too. He only has a few days.
The local neighborhood board has called an emergency meeting
Thursday evening. If John can present facts and evidence, maybe
he can stop this outbreak. Maybe he can save lives.

It all comes down to evidence.

Monday morning. John's back on Broad Street. This time, he knocks on doors.

We can guess the hard questions he must ask: *Did anyone in your family drink water from the Broad Street pump last week? Did the person who drank the water get sick?*

John's not surprised to find that people who got cholera *did* drink the water. But he's looking for exceptions, too. *Who hasn't gotten sick—and why not?*

He finds one exception at the Lion Brewery, where not a single worker has died. These men breathe the same air as everyone else on Broad Street. But they have their own water source (and drink lots of ale as well!). They don't drink water from the pump. This fact is helpful. But it's not enough to change people's minds.

So John keeps searching. On Tuesday, he heads to the London records office to get a list of those who've lost their lives. Then John visits more families. He keeps knocking on doors, asking questions, and gathering facts. All the while, cholera is spreading. Time is running out.

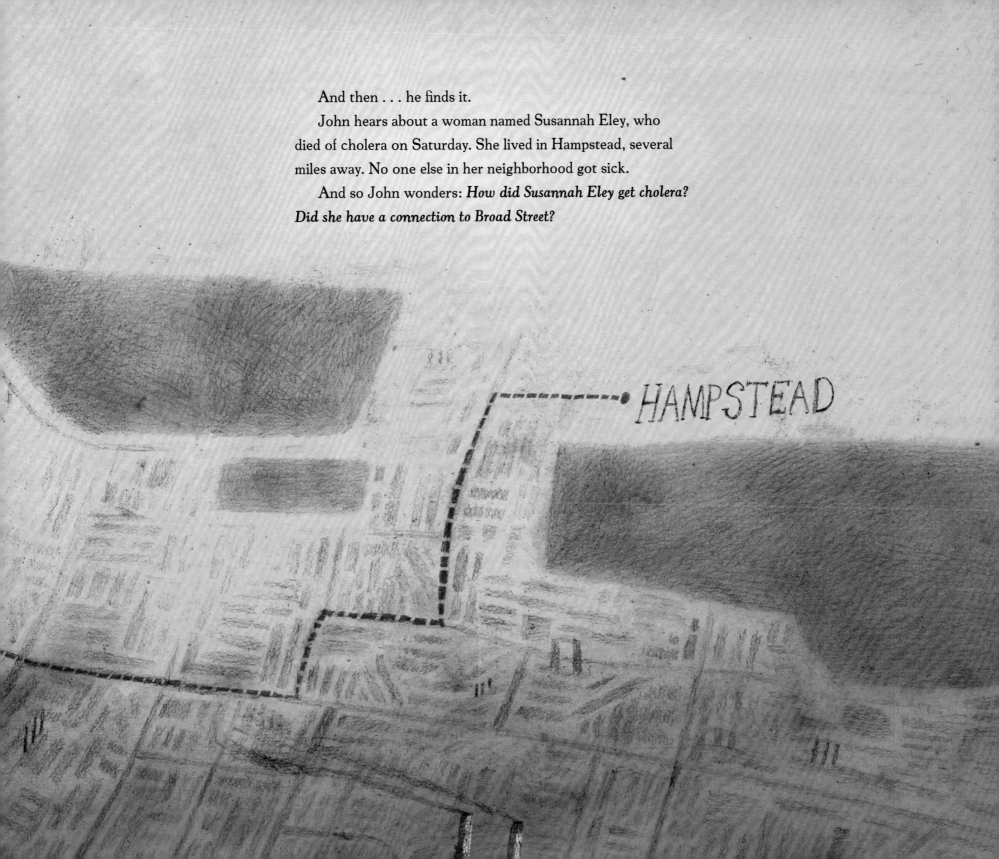

And then . . . he finds it.

John hears about a woman named Susannah Eley, who died of cholera on Saturday. She lived in Hampstead, several miles away. No one else in her neighborhood got sick.

And so John wonders: *How did Susannah Eley get cholera? Did she have a connection to Broad Street?*

HAMPSTEAD

Eley . . . the name is familiar.
John sees there's an Eley family factory on
Broad Street. It's now run by Susannah's sons.
Before she retired to a house a few miles away,
Susannah Eley always got her water from the
Broad Street pump. So now her devoted sons
send her a jug of it each week.

Oh, what a hard question John has to ask: *Did you send your mum water last week?*
By now you can guess the heartbreaking answer: Yes!
It's the proof John's been so desperate to find. Susannah Eley got cholera by
drinking water from the Broad Street pump.

Armed with this strong evidence, John attends the Thursday-night meeting.
He makes his case. We can imagine his urgent appeal: *Please take the handle
off the Broad Street pump. We can't cure cholera, but we can help stop it from
spreading. We can help keep children and families safe.*

The committee isn't sure John's right. But his idea is their only hope. They say yes.

The very next day—Friday, September 8, 1854—the handle is removed from the Broad Street pump. It's a milestone in science, a shining moment in the long fight against epidemics.

And it all came down to **evidence**.

THE CASE AGAINST THE BROAD STREET PUMP

Evidence! is a true story that marks a key date in public health history: September 8, 1854, when the handle came off the Broad Street pump in London, England. A few months later, Dr. John Snow published a book about his investigation that included a map showing the pattern of the epidemic. This map has inspired scientists ever since.

The outbreak killed 616 people. Even after it ended, John and Rev. Henry Whitehead, a neighborhood priest, kept searching for evidence of how it began. They found it! Death certificates showed that Annie Lewis's baby sister, Frances, was the first to get sick. It turned out that her mom, Sarah, rinsed out the baby's diapers in a cesspool (tank) in the cellar. When workers dug down, they found leaks that allowed human waste to seep from the cesspool into the dirt—and then into the Broad Street pump well, just a few feet away.

Annie's dad got sick the same day the pump handle came off. Until he died on September 19, his wife emptied buckets of human waste into the cesspool. If the handle hadn't come off, people would have kept drinking the contaminated water. Thanks to Dr. John Snow, no one did.

DR. JOHN SNOW (1813 - 1858)

Dr. John Snow is often called the father of modern epidemiology. Epidemiologists study how diseases spread and use facts and evidence to help keep people safe. John was born on March 15, 1813, in York, England, the eldest of nine children. John started his medical training as an apprentice when he was only fourteen. He treated his first cholera patients when still a teen.

John moved to London in 1836 to continue his medical education and set up a practice. Along with his research on cholera, John was a leader in the new field of anesthesiology, using substances like chloroform to relieve pain. He even treated Queen Victoria!

Although John published his book about the Broad Street outbreak in 1855, it took until 1866 before people fully accepted his conclusion that cholera was a water-borne disease. Sadly, John was not there to see it. He died of a stroke on June 16, 1858. But John's legacy lives on. Each year, the John Snow Society invites a leading scientist to give a lecture on public health. The event is called the Pumphandle Lecture.

MAJOR INFECTIOUS DISEASES AND THEIR CAUSES

Dr. John Snow is just one of the many dedicated scientists, past and present, whose work has helped to save lives. Here is what research and evidence tells us about other major infectious diseases.

Cholera bacterium, *Vibrio cholerae (V. cholerae)*

Cholera is usually transmitted when people drink contaminated water. Cholera is more common when natural disasters disrupt water supplies or in areas without clean water and sanitation.

Coronavirus Disease (Covid-19) virus (coronavirus called SARS-CoV-2)

The World Health Organization (WHO) declared Covid-19 a global pandemic beginning in March 2020. WHO announced in May 2023 that the emergency phase had ended. Coronavirus particles spread through the air from an infected person's mouth or nose through speaking, sneezing, etc. Vaccines help prevent severe infections.

HIV virus (human immunodeficiency virus)

HIV attacks a person's immune system. There is no cure, but long-term treatments help to lessen HIV's severity. HIV is spread from genital fluids, blood, or breast milk. Its most advanced stage is AIDS, acquired immunodeficiency syndrome.

Influenza virus (A and B influenza viruses)

From 1918 to 1920, a flu virus caused a global pandemic that killed up to fifty million people. Each year, various subtypes of flu viruses circulate. Scientists develop annual vaccines to lessen symptoms and prevent transmission.

Malaria parasites, esp. *Plasmodium falciparum* and *Plasmodium vivax*

People get malaria parasites when they're bitten by an infected *Anopheles* mosquito. In 2021, WHO reported nearly 250 million cases and about 600,000 deaths, primarily among children in sub-Saharan Africa. Controlling mosquito populations via nets, repellants, and other measures helps prevent infection.

Plague bacterium, *Yersinia pestis (Y. pestis)*

People get infected by plague bacteria from an infected animal (such as a marmot or rat), through an agent, or vector, like a flea. During the fourteenth century, plague killed millions in the Great Mortality. It's now treated with antibiotics.

Polio virus (poliovirus)

Poliomyelitis is a disease that destroys nerve cells in the spinal cord and can cause paralysis. It spreads when people come into contact with small particles of fecal matter (poop), perhaps in a swimming pool or lake, or by changing the diaper of an infected baby and not washing their hands right away. Polio cases in the United States declined in the 1950s after Dr. Jonas Salk developed a vaccine. WHO is working toward the global eradication of polio.

Smallpox virus (variola virus)

Smallpox is the only communicable, or infectious, disease to have been completely eradicated through a global vaccination campaign. It caused millions of deaths over a period of 3,000 years.

INTERNET RESOURCES

Dr. John Snow website at the UCLA Fielding School of Public Health
ph.ucla.edu/epi/snow.html
The John Snow Society (including John's famous Broad Street disease map)
johnsnowsociety.org

BOOKS ABOUT DR. JOHN SNOW

Hempel, Sandra. *The Strange Case of the Broad Street Pump: John Snow and the Mystery of Cholera.* Berkeley: University of California Press, 2007.

Johnson, Steven. *The Ghost Map: The Story of London's Most Terrifying Epidemic—and How It Changed Science, Cities, and the Modern World.* New York: Riverhead Books, 2006.

BOOKS FOR YOUNG READERS ABOUT EPIDEMICS

Anderson, Laurie Halse. *Fever 1793.* New York: Simon & Schuster Books for Young Readers, 2000.

Barnard, Bryn. *Outbreak! Plagues That Changed History.* New York: Crown, 2005.

Farrell, Jeannette. *Invisible Enemies: Stories of Infectious Diseases.* New York: Farrar, Straus and Giroux, 2005.

Hopkinson, Deborah. *The Deadliest Diseases Then and Now.* New York: Scholastic Focus, 2021.

Murphy, Jim. *An American Plague: The True and Terrifying Story of the Yellow Fever Epidemic of 1793.* New York: Clarion Books, 2003.

To epidemiologists and health-care workers the world over —D.H.

For my mother, a fantastic nurse —N.H.

THIS IS A BORZOI BOOK PUBLISHED BY ALFRED A. KNOPF
Text copyright © 2024 by Deborah Hopkinson
Jacket art and interior illustrations copyright © 2024 by Nik Henderson
All rights reserved. Published in the United States by Alfred A. Knopf,
an imprint of Random House Children's Books, a division of Penguin Random House LLC, New York.
Knopf, Borzoi Books, and the colophon are registered trademarks of Penguin Random House LLC.

Visit us on the Web! rhcbooks.com
Educators and librarians, for a variety of teaching tools, visit us at RHTeachersLibrarians.com

Library of Congress Cataloging-in-Publication Data is available upon request.
ISBN 978-0-593-42681-4 (hardcover) — ISBN 978-0-593-42682-1 (lib. bdg.) — ISBN 978-0-593-42683-8 (ebook)

The text of this book is set in 13-point Cooper Old Style.
The illustrations were created using graphite, charcoal, and digital coloring techniques.
Interior design by Sarah Hokanson

MANUFACTURED IN CHINA 10 9 8 7 6 5 4 3 2 1 First Edition